SICS

*Great American
Short Stories I*

⤣⤦

Nathaniel
HAWTHORNE

Stories retold by Emily Hutchinson
Illustrated by James McConnell

LAKE EDUCATION
Belmont, California

LAKE CLASSICS

Great American Short Stories I

Washington Irving, Nathaniel Hawthorne, Mark Twain, Bret
Harte, Edgar Allan Poe, Kate Chopin, Willa Cather, Sarah
Orne Jewett, Sherwood Anderson, Charles W. Chesnutt

Great American Short Stories II

Herman Melville, Stephen Crane, Ambrose Bierce, Jack
London, Edith Wharton, Charlotte Perkins Gilman, Frank R.
Stockton, Hamlin Garland, O. Henry, Richard Harding Davis

Great British and Irish Short Stories

Arthur Conan Doyle, Saki (H. H. Munro), Rudyard Kipling,
Katherine Mansfield, Thomas Hardy, E. M. Forster, Robert
Louis Stevenson, H. G. Wells, John Galsworthy, James Joyce

Great Short Stories from Around the World

Guy de Maupassant, Anton Chekhov, Leo Tolstoy, Selma
Lagerlöf, Alphonse Daudet, Mori Ogwai, Leopoldo Alas,
Rabindranath Tagore, Fyodor Dostoevsky, Honoré de Balzac

Cover and Text Designer: Diann Abbott

Library of Congress Catalog Number: 94-075013
ISBN 1-56103-003-1
Printed in the United States of America
1 9 8 7 6 5 4 3 2 1

CONTENTS

❧ Lake Classic Short Stories ❧

"The universe is made of stories, not atoms."

—Muriel Rukeyser

"The story's about you."

—Horace

Everyone loves a good story. It is hard to think of a friendlier introduction to classic literature. For one thing, short stories are *short*—quick to get into and easy to finish. Of all the literary forms, the short story is the least intimidating and the most approachable.

Great literature is an important part of our human heritage. In the belief that this heritage belongs to everyone, *Lake Classic Short Stories* are adapted for today's readers. Lengthy sentences and paragraphs are shortened. Archaic words are replaced. Modern punctuation and spellings are used. Many of the longer stories are abridged. In all the stories,

5

painstaking care has been taken to preserve the author's unique voice.

Lake Classic Short Stories have something for everyone. The hundreds of stories in the collection cover a broad terrain of themes, story types, and styles. Literary merit was a deciding factor in story selection. But no story was included unless it was as enjoyable as it was instructive. And special priority was given to stories that shine light on the human condition.

Each book in the *Lake Classic Short Stories* is devoted to the work of a single author. Little-known stories of merit are included with famous old favorites. Taken as a whole, the collected authors and stories make up a rich and diverse sampler of the story-teller's art.

Lake Classic Short Stories guarantee a great reading experience. Readers who look for common interests, concerns, and experiences are sure to find them. Readers who bring their own gifts of perception and appreciation to the stories will be doubly rewarded.

❦ Nathaniel Hawthorne ❦
(1804–1864)

About the Author

Nathaniel Hawthorne was born in Salem, Massachusetts, on the Fourth of July in 1804. He died suddenly, while on a walking tour, in the year before the Civil War ended.

Hawthorne lived during a rich period of American literature known as the American Renaissance. Among his neighbors and friends were such famous writers as Ralph Waldo Emerson, Henry David Thoreau, and Herman Melville. It was Melville who said that Hawthorne had the "great power of blackness." This meant that he understood the dark inner landscape—the sorrow, guilt, sin, and loneliness of the human mind. The central theme of Hawthorne's work was sin, and how people pay for it.

Hawthorne was the second of three children. His father was a sea captain who died of yellow fever when the boy was only four. One of his ancestors was a judge in the Salem Witch Trials of 1692. All of his life Hawthorne felt the weight of this Puritan heritage.

Hawthorne's first collection of short stories was published in 1837. But this book brought him neither fame nor money, so he took a job in the Boston Custom House. Success was slow in coming. He once wrote a children's history of the world that sold over a million copies. All he got for it was $100.

Hawthorne's greatness was not recognized until *The Scarlet Letter*, his masterpiece, was published in 1850. From 1853 to 1860, Hawthorne worked and traveled in England and Italy.

To Hawthorne, isolation from society was the greatest punishment. In a letter to a friend, Hawthorne once said, "There is no fate in the world so horrible as to have no share in either its joys or sorrows." If you enjoy stories with a moral twist, you will enjoy Nathaniel Hawthorne.

The Birthmark

Which is stronger—the young doctor's fascination with science or his love for his wife? This is a story about arrogance, pride, and conflicting values. The question it raises is still being asked today: Can science always win out against Mother Nature?

"GEORGINA, DID YOU EVER THINK THAT THE BIRTHMARK
ON YOUR CHEEK MIGHT BE TAKEN OFF?"

The Birthmark

Not long before our story opens, a brilliant scientist fell in love with a beautiful woman. Because of this, he left an assistant to take care of his work. He washed the smoke of the lab from his face. He cleaned the stain of acids from his fingers. Then he asked the woman to become his wife.

Now, in those days, electricity had only just been discovered. This and other new discoveries of science seemed to be like miracles. So it was not unusual for the love of science to be very strong. Perhaps it was even as strong as the love between a man and a woman.

We do not know if Aylmer thought that human beings could control Nature. But he was a very good scientist, and he had always loved his work. His love for his young wife *might* prove to be stronger than his love for science. But it seemed that both of these loves would have to live side by side.

In fact, these loves *did* live side by side in Aylmer. The end result was truly remarkable. And the lesson to be learned is interesting.

One day, soon after the marriage, Aylmer sat looking at his wife. Finally, he spoke aloud about what had been bothering him.

"Georgiana, did you ever think that the birthmark on your cheek might be taken off?" he asked.

"No, indeed," she said, smiling. "In fact, it has often been called charming. I was foolish enough to think that was true."

"Ah! On some other face it might be charming. But not on yours. No, dear Georgiana! You are so very close to being perfect that this mark always comes to me as a shock."

"A shock, my dear husband!" cried Georgiana, very hurt. First she got red with anger, and then she started crying. "Then why did you take me from my mother's side? You cannot love someone who shocks you!"

In the center of Georgiana's left cheek was a small red birthmark. It was easy to see most of the time, when her face was pale. But when she blushed, the mark became harder to see. If any feelings made her turn white, the mark would show up again.

The birthmark looked like a red patch on snow. It was shaped like a very small human hand. People who loved Georgiana said that an angel had put her hand on Georgiana's cheek when she was born. Many men would have risked their lives just to kiss that mark.

Other people thought that the mark made Georgiana look ugly. Some men thought that everything else about

Georgiana was beautiful. They wished the mark were gone. If it were, they thought, there would be one person in the world who was completely perfect. After his marriage, Aylmer found that this was how he felt.

If Georgiana had been less beautiful, it might not have mattered to Aylmer. But because she was perfect except for this, the birthmark began to haunt him.

At the times when the young couple should have been happiest, he thought again and again about the mark on her face. As small as it was, it became the most important thing in Aylmer's mind. In the morning, Aylmer opened his eyes, looked at his wife's face, and saw the mark. When they sat together in the evening, he looked only at the mark. Georgiana soon learned to shudder at his gaze. When she saw that he was staring at the mark, her face would lose all color. Then the mark would stand out even more.

One evening when the light was growing dim, she brought up the subject. "Do you remember, my dear Aylmer," she said, "if you have ever dreamed about this terrible birthmark?"

"Never!" said Aylmer. But then he said, "I don't know why I never dreamed of it— for I think of it often."

"Are you sure you did not dream of it last night?" asked Georgiana. "It must have been a terrible dream. Think! You said, 'It is in her heart now. We must have it out!' Think, my husband! I want you to remember that dream."

Suddenly Aylmer *did* remember the dream. In his dream, he had been with his servant, Aminadab. He was operating on Georgiana, trying hard to remove the birthmark. The deeper the knife went, the deeper his hand sank. Finally, the knife seemed to catch hold of Georgiana's heart.

As he remembered the dream, Aylmer looked away from his wife, feeling guilty.

Until that moment, he had not realized how important the birthmark was to him. He had not realized how far he might go to get rid of it.

"Aylmer," said Georgiana, "I do not know what it may cost both us to rid me of this mark. If it is removed, I may look even worse. Perhaps the mark goes as deep as life itself. Again, I ask you, do you know of any way to get rid of it?"

"Dearest Georgiana," he said, "I have thought a great deal about this. I am sure that I can remove the mark."

"If there is even the smallest chance, then try it," said Georgiana. "Danger means nothing to me. As long as this mark is ugly to you, then I will gladly risk my life to get rid of it. Either take this mark away, or take away my miserable life!

"You are a fine scientist. The whole world knows it. You have done great things. Surely you can remove this tiny mark! Do it—for the sake of your own peace, and to save your poor wife from madness."

"Dear, sweet wife," cried Aylmer, "do not think that I can't do it! I have already given this matter the deepest thought. You have led me even deeper into the heart of science. Georgiana, I know that I can do it. Afterwards, my most beloved, your dear cheek will be as perfect as the other cheek. You will be the most nearly perfect woman on earth!"

"It is settled, then," said Georgiana. "And Aylmer—even if you find that the mark has its roots in my heart, take it out."

Then her husband kissed her cheek— her right cheek, not the one that had the mark.

The next day, Aylmer told his wife of his plan. They would both move into Aylmer's lab. They would not leave until Aylmer had discovered a way to remove the mark. As he led her into the lab, Georgiana was cold and shaking. Aylmer looked into her face, thinking he would cheer her up. But he was so surprised to see how bright the birthmark was on her white cheek that he shuddered. His wife fainted.

"Aminadab! Aminadab!" shouted Aylmer. In answer, a short man hurried from an inner room. He had long hair hanging around his face, which was dirty from the smoke of the lab. This man had been Aylmer's helper during his whole career. His strong body and mechanical mind seemed to represent the physical side of human beings. Aylmer, on the other hand, with his slim body and his pale face, seemed to represent the spiritual side.

"Open the door of the bedroom, Aminadab," said Aylmer. "Burn some incense to help her wake up."

"Yes, master," said Aminadab, looking at the still body of Georgiana. Then he said to himself, "If she were my wife, I'd leave that mark alone."

When Georgiana woke up, she found herself breathing a strange odor. The room was quite beautiful. Aylmer had decorated it very nicely. The walls were hung from ceiling to floor with gorgeous curtains. He had put perfumed lamps all around the room.

Now Aylmer knelt by his wife's side. He watched her carefully, but there was no worry in his eyes. He was sure that his science could draw a magic circle around her, and that no evil could get in.

"Where am I? Ah, now I remember," said Georgiana. Then she put her hand over her cheek. More than anything she wanted to hide the terrible mark from her husband's eyes.

"Fear not, dear one!" he said. "Do not hide from me. Believe me, Georgiana, I am only happy that I will soon be able to remove that one flaw in your beauty."

"Oh, spare me!" said his wife, sadly. "Please do not look at it again. ·I can never forget how you shudder when you look at it."

To calm Georgiana down and to entertain her, Aylmer decided to perform some scientific tricks. First he showed her some moving pictures. Now, moving pictures were such a new thing at that time that it seemed almost magic. When she got tired of this, Aylmer told her to look at a small pot of soil. She did so, with little interest at first. Then she looked more closely and saw a plant shooting up. First came the slim stalk. Then the leaves slowly grew. Finally, a perfect, lovely flower appeared.

"It is magic!" cried Georgiana. "I dare not touch it."

"No, pick it from the stem. Pick it, and breathe in its perfume while you may. The flower will die in a few minutes and leave nothing but its seeds. But other flowers just as lovely may be grown from those plain brown seeds."

As soon as Georgiana touched the flower, it died. Its leaves turned as black as if they had been burned by fire.

"Your touch was too strong," said Aylmer.

To make up for this, Aylmer decided to take her picture. This, too, was a new scientific process. Aylmer had invented a way to focus rays of light on a polished metal plate to make a picture. But when she looked at the picture, she was disappointed. The features of her face were fuzzy, but the birthmark itself was very clear. Aylmer grabbed the picture and threw it into a jar of acid.

Then Aylmer began to talk to Georgiana about the wonders of science. He told her that he could make a liquid that could make people live much longer. They might, in fact, live forever. But then he said that the people who drank the liquid might not, in the end, be happy about it.

"Aylmer, are you telling the truth?" asked Georgiana, looking at him in fear. "It is terrible to have such power—or even to dream of it."

"Oh, do not be afraid, my love," said her husband. "I would not try such a thing on either you or myself. I only tell you this so you can understand what a good scientist I am. It will be easy for me to remove your birthmark."

As soon as Aylmer spoke about her birthmark, Georgiana again grew fearful. She felt as if a red-hot iron had touched her cheek.

Aylmer went back to his work. She could hear him talking to Aminadab in the furnace room. Soon he came back to her side and showed her a small bottle. In it was a gentle yet very powerful fragrance. Aylmer said it could change the aroma of all the breezes that blow across a country. As he spoke, he threw some of the perfume into the air. It filled the room with a delightful smell.

"And what is this?" asked Georgiana. She pointed to a small glass full of golden liquid. "What a beautiful color! I could imagine it to be the liquid of life itself."

"In one sense it is," said Aylmer. "Rather, it is the liquid of eternal life. It is the most valuable liquid that ever was made in this world. By using it, I could determine how long anyone might live. The amount of the dose would tell whether the person would live many years, or die in the middle of a breath. No king on his throne could live if I decided that it would be better if he died."

"Why do you keep such a terrible liquid?" asked Georgiana, in horror.

"Do not think I would ever use it, dearest," said her husband, smiling. "Even so, it could be used for good as easily as it could be used for evil. But look! Here is a strong cosmetic. Just a few drops of this in a vase of water is all it takes. Then freckles can be washed away as easily as the hands are washed. A few more drops would take the blood out of the cheek. It would leave the rosiest beauty a pale ghost."

"Is this what you plan to use on my cheek?" asked Georgiana.

"Oh, no," said her husband. "This only works on the surface. Your case needs a medicine that will go deeper."

As he spoke to his wife, Aylmer often asked her if she felt comfortable. He asked if the temperature of the air agreed with her. He asked so many questions that Georgiana began to think that he was already treating her.

Perhaps she had breathed in some medicine with the fragrant air. Perhaps she had eaten some in her food. She felt a strange stirring in her body. She had an odd creeping feeling in her veins. This feeling tingled at her heart—half painfully and half pleasurably. Still, whenever she looked in the mirror, she saw that the red birthmark had not faded from her cheek. She hated it now even more than Aylmer did.

To pass the time, she started to read some of the books in her husband's library. Of all his books, the one she found most interesting was written by Aylmer himself. In his own handwriting, he had kept records of every experiment he had ever done. This book was truly the history and symbol of his whole life.

As she read, Georgiana felt greater love than ever for Aylmer. Yet she began to realize that even he made mistakes. As much as he had accomplished—she could not help but notice that he usually fell short of his goals. On the one hand, the book told of all the successes that had brought the man fame. On the other hand, it also told of his pain at not accomplishing more. Perhaps any great genius might have these same experiences.

Georgiana was deeply moved. She laid her face on the open book and burst into tears. This is how she was found by Aylmer.

"It is dangerous to read a sorcerer's books," he said. He was smiling at her, even though his face looked uneasy and displeased. "Georgiana, there are pages in that book that I can barely read myself. I, too, find them upsetting. Be careful. Don't let what you read upset you."

"It has made me worship you even more," said Georgiana.

"Ah, just wait for this one success," he said. "Then you may worship me if you like. When your birthmark is gone, I might even feel worthy of it. But come, I have been looking for you so I could hear you sing. Sing to me, dearest."

So she poured out the liquid music of her voice to quench the thirst of his spirit. He then went back to his work in a happy mood. He assured her that her treatment was working, and that the birthmark would soon be gone. As soon as he left, Georgiana decided to follow him. She had forgotten to tell him about a strange thing that had been happening for the past two hours. It was a *feeling* in the birthmark. It was not painful, but somehow it made her restless. Hurrying after her husband, she went for the first time into his lab.

The first thing she noticed was the red-hot furnace. It looked as if it had been burning for ages. Scattered around the room were all sorts of bottles, tubes, and other items used in scientific research. The heavy air was full of chemical odors. But what she noticed most of all was Aylmer himself.

Her husband was pale as death, and extremely absorbed in his work. He leaned over the furnace, anxiously watching the liquid he was working with.

He seemed like a different person than the one who had just left Georgiana.

"Carefully now, Aminadab. Carefully. Now, if there is but a drop too much or too little, it is all over."

"Ho! Ho!" said Aminadab. "Look, master! Look!"

Aylmer raised his eyes quickly. When he saw Georgiana, his face first got red and then grew pale. He rushed toward her and grabbed her arm. He held her arm so tightly that he left the print of his fingers on it.

"Why did you come here? Have you no trust in your husband?" he cried. "Would you throw the curse of that birthmark over my work? This is not good. Go, woman, go!"

"No, Aylmer," said Georgiana firmly. "You have no right to complain. You are the one who lacks trust. You have been keeping from me the problems in this experiment. Do not think so little of me, my husband. Tell me about the risk we run. Do not be afraid that I will back out. My share in this experiment is far less than your own. I shall drink whatever liquid you bring me. I shall do it for the same reason that I would take poison if you gave it to me."

Aylmer was deeply moved. "My noble wife," he said, "I did not know how strong you were until now. Nothing shall be hidden. Know, then, that your birthmark—as small as it seems—is very strong. I have already given you medicines powerful enough to change your entire physical system. There is only one thing left to try. It that fails, we are ruined."

"Why didn't you tell me this before?" she asked.

"Because, Georgiana," said Aylmer in a low voice, "there is danger."

"Danger? There is only one danger— that this horrible mark shall be left on my cheek!" cried Georgiana. "Remove it, remove it, whatever the cost may be, or we shall both go mad!"

"Heaven knows your words are too true," said Aylmer, sadly. "And now, dearest, return to your room. In a little while, all will be tested."

He took her back and left her with a solemn tenderness. After he left, Georgiana began to think about Aylmer and how much she loved him. She was grateful for his love. It must be high and pure indeed—for he would accept nothing less than perfection. She thought that only a man who loved her less would have accepted her birthmark. She wished only that she could be worthy of his love.

Then the sound of her husband's footsteps broke into her thoughts. He was carrying a crystal glass full of a liquid as colorless as water. Aylmer was pale, but it seemed to be the result of hard work rather than of fear or doubt.

"This liquid is perfect," he said, in answer to Georgiana's look. "Unless all my science has fooled me, it cannot fail."

"And if it does fail," said Georgiana, "I am ready to die."

"Why do you speak of dying? This liquid cannot fail. Look what it does to this plant."

Near the window was a sick geranium. It had yellow spots all over its leaves. Aylmer poured a small amount of the liquid on the soil in the pot. As soon as the roots of the plant got wet, the yellow spots all turned a healthy, bright green.

"You didn't have to prove anything to me," said Georgiana. "Give me the glass. I joyfully risk everything on your word."

"Drink, then!" exclaimed Aylmer. "Your spirit is perfect. Soon your body shall be perfect as well!"

She drank the liquid and returned the glass to his hand. "It tastes like water from a heavenly fountain. Now, dearest, let me sleep. My earthly senses are closing over my spirit like the leaves around the heart of a rose at sunset."

But she spoke as if talking took too much energy. As soon as she said these words, she was lost in sleep. Aylmer sat by her side, watching her carefully. He watched as if his own life depended on what happened. He noticed the slightest flush on her cheek. He noticed every breath she took, every movement of her eyelid, every change in position. All these were details written down in his book.

He gazed at the birthmark, not without a shudder. Yet once, by a strange desire, he pressed it with his lips. As he continued to watch, the birthmark began to grow fainter. Imagine the colors of the rainbow fading out of the sky. The fading of the birthmark was something like that.

"By Heaven! It is almost gone!" said Aylmer to himself. "I can barely see it now. Success! Success! And now it is like the faintest rose color. The slightest amount of color in her face would hide it. But she is so pale!"

He opened the curtains and allowed the light of day to fall into the room. The light rested on her cheek. At the same time, he heard Aminadab laugh in delight.

"Ah, Aminadab!" said Aylmer. "You have served me well. Matter and spirit— earth and heaven—both have done their part in this! Laugh, Aminadab! You have earned the right to laugh!"

This noise woke Georgiana. Slowly she opened her eyes and looked into the mirror. A faint smile flitted across her lips when she saw that the birthmark was so faint. But then she gazed at Aylmer with a troubled look.

"My poor Aylmer!" she said.

"Poor? No—richest, happiest, most favored!" he said. "My beautiful bride, it is successful! You are perfect!"

"My poor Aylmer," she repeated, with a more than human tenderness. "You have aimed high, you have done well. Do not be sorry that you have rejected the best the earth could offer. Aylmer, dearest Aylmer, I am dying!"

Alas! It was true. The birthmark had been the bond by which an angelic spirit was united to a human body. The last red tint of the birthmark faded from Georgiana's cheek. At the same time, the last breath of the now perfect woman passed into the air.

The Threefold Destiny

Have you ever looked for the right thing in the wrong place? In this story a man in search of his destiny comes back home disappointed. Nowhere in the world has he found what he was looking for. Should he give up on his dreams? Or should he take a closer look at his own hometown?

"NOW, A FOOLISH MAN MIGHT THINK THE TREASURE LIES BURIED AT THE VERY DOOR OF HIS MOTHER'S HOUSE."

The Threefold Destiny

One summer evening, a tall, dark figure entered a village not far from here. The man had been traveling in faraway places for a long time. He carried with him many things from other lands.

The walking stick that this traveler used had come from the jungles of Hindustan. The hat he was wearing had protected him from the suns of Spain. His cheek had felt the red-hot wind of an Arabian desert—as well as the frozen breath of the Arctic. He had traveled for a long time among wild and dangerous men. And he still carried the long knife that he had used as protection against robbers.

Moving from country to country, he had lost some of his New England habits. He had picked up many new habits from all around the world. So when this world traveler came home, it is no wonder that people didn't recognize him. That doesn't mean that no one noticed him. Everyone was curious about who this stranger was, although no one could place him at first.

Then, as he walked through the village, his arm casually touched the arm of a young woman who was passing by. She was on her way to an evening lecture. As she looked at him, she almost cried out.

"Ralph Cranfield!" was the name that she nearly said.

"Can that be my old playmate, Faith Egerton?" thought the traveler. He looked around, but he did not stop.

From the time he was young, Ralph Cranfield had thought he was marked for great things. For some reason, he had the idea that three marvelous events would happen to him. Each one, he thought, would be announced to him by a special sign.

The first of these events was the one that he thought about most fondly. This was to be the discovery of the one maiden on earth whose love could make him happy. He was to roam around the world until he would meet a beautiful woman wearing a certain jewel. This jewel would be in the shape of a heart. It didn't matter if the jewel was a pearl, ruby, emerald, opal, or diamond. Ralph Cranfield didn't care, so long as it was in the shape of a heart.

On meeting this lovely stranger, he would say, "Maiden, I have brought you a heavy heart. May I rest its weight on you?" If she were the woman of his dreams, she would touch the heart-shaped jewel as she answered. She would say, "This heart, which I have worn so long, is the sign that you may."

Secondly, Ralph Cranfield believed that a great treasure was hidden somewhere in the earth. He thought that the burial place of this treasure would be shown only to him. When he stood on the mysterious spot, a hand would appear before him. The hand would be pointing downward. He did not know if the hand would be carved of marble or cut out of the side of a mountain. It might even be shaped by flames in empty air. He only knew that it would be a hand, the finger pointing downward. Under it would be the Latin word *Effode*—Dig! He would dig there, and the treasure would be his.

There was one more miraculous event that Ralph Cranfield thought would happen to him. He felt that he would someday have great influence over other people. Perhaps he would be a king on a throne. Perhaps he would be a leader of people fighting for their freedom. Perhaps he would be the apostle of a new faith. He did not know how, but he was sure that he was destined for greatness. The sign of this third and last event would be that three honored men would ask to see him. The wisest one, dressed in flowing garments, would be holding a wand or a prophet's rod. With this wand or rod, the wise man would trace a message in the air. If Ralph obeyed the message, it would lead to glorious results.

In his youth, Ralph Cranfield had set forth from the village with this wonderful future before him. He was on his way to seek the maid, the treasure, and the wise man. But had he found them? Alas! It was not as a successful man that Ralph was returning to his home. Rather, he was returning with the gloom of a person who had had very bad luck. He had not come back home to stay. His wish was only that he might regain his youthful hope before leaving once more.

Ralph saw that there had been few changes in the village. The elm trees were larger. The houses had more moss on them. The cemetery had a few more gravestones. Yet, even though ten years had passed, it seemed almost as if Ralph Cranfield had left that very morning. His heart grew cold because the village did not seem to remember him as well as he remembered it.

"Here is the biggest change," he sighed, striking his hand to his heart. "Who is this old and worried man, heavy with disappointed hopes? The young man who went forth so joyously is gone forever!"

And now Ralph Cranfield was at his mother's gate. He let himself into the front yard and made friends again with the tree of his childhood. As he leaned against the old tree, he noticed something on the trunk. It was a carving that he had made long ago. It had taken him a whole day to carve the Latin word *Effode* in the bark of the tree. Now, looking at this carving, he smiled sadly.

How odd it was that the bark just above the word had put forth a new growth! It was shaped something like a hand. The finger was pointing downward. Such, at least, was how it appeared in the dusky light.

"Now, a foolish man might think that the treasure lies buried at the very door of my mother's house. And I have been looking all over the world for it! That would really be a good joke!" thought Ralph Cranfield.

He thought no more about it, for the door swung open. An elderly woman came through the doorway. She peered into the dusk to see who had come into her yard. It was Ralph Cranfield's mother. We will pass over their greeting, and leave the one to her joy and the other to his rest.

When morning broke, Ralph Cranfield arose with a troubled heart. The whole night had been full of dreams. His childhood dreams seemed to have been waiting for him beneath his mother's roof. In his old bedroom, he had passed a wilder night than he ever had in an Arab tent. It was even wilder than when he had slept in a haunted forest.

In his dream, a shadowy maid had come to his bedside and put her finger on his beating heart. A hand of flame had glowed in the darkness, pointing downward. A white-haired wise man had waved a wand and called the dreamer forward.

These same dreams, though fainter in the daylight, still lived in the cottage. They joined the crowd of familiar faces that came to the cottage to welcome Ralph Cranfield home.

Meanwhile, his mother was full of joy that she again had somebody to love and care for. It was nearly noon when she looked outside and saw three important men coming along the street. Finally, they reached her gate and opened it.

"See, Ralph!" she exclaimed. "Here is Squire Hawkwood and the two other officials of the village. They've come just to see you! Now do tell them a good story about what you have seen in foreign parts."

The first of the three visitors, Squire Hawkwood, was an excellent old gentleman. No one doubted that he was the most important man in the village. Many people in the village thought he was one of the wisest men on earth. Every day the Squire wore a fancy three-cornered hat and carried a silver-headed cane. He used the cane more for waving in the air than for helping himself to walk.

His two companions were elderly and respected officials. They walked slightly behind Squire Hawkwood, out of respect for his greater station. As they came up to the cottage door, Ralph Cranfield wondered what their visit meant.

"Here come three elderly men," he thought, smiling to himself. "The first of the three is an honorable wise man carrying a staff. What if this group should bring me the message about my fate!"

As the men entered the cottage, Ralph greeted them. The Squire gave an elaborate flourish with his cane in the air. Then he removed his hat and finally began to speak.

"My colleagues and I," began the Squire, "have been worried for three days. We need to find just the right person to fill a very special position. This person will take upon himself a job that is as important as that of a king. We have finally decided that you are the best person for this job."

During this speech, Cranfield gazed at the Squire. He almost imagined that the Squire was wearing the flowing robes of an ancient wise man. Indeed, the Squire had waved his cane in the air before beginning to speak. This was exactly the signal of the wise man that Cranfield had been seeking around the world.

"And what," asked Ralph Cranfield, with a shaking in his voice, "is this job that is equal to that of a king?"

"No less than instructor of our village school," answered Squire Hawkwood. "Master Whitaker, after 50 years as our teacher, has recently died. That leaves the position open."

"I will consider your kind offer," said Ralph, quickly. "I will let you know within three days."

After a few more words, the three men left. But in Cranfield's imagination, they were still there. He thought about the Squire and got him confused in his mind with the wise man of his dreams. One seemed to be but a shadow of the other. The same face, he now thought, had looked on him from a great pyramid in

Egypt. And he had seen the face in other places around the world.

All day Ralph Cranfield sat in the cottage, thinking. He barely heard his mother's thousand questions about his travels and adventures. At sunset, he left the house to take a little walk. When he passed the elm tree, his eye was again caught by the image of a hand. It was pointing downward at the words in the bark.

As he walked through the village, he remembered every turn in the pathway. A group of cows was grazing on the grassy roadside. He could smell their fragrant breath. "It is sweeter than the perfumes of the Spice Islands," he thought. The round little figure of a child rolled from a doorway. The child lay laughing almost at Cranfield's feet. He bent over, lifted the child, and put him back in his mother's arms. "The children," he said to himself, "are to be my charge." He sighed and smiled.

He continued his walk and passed by a cottage. From within, he heard a sweet voice, humming a song. The song seemed to come from a deep and tender soul.

He bent his head and entered the cottage, just as a young woman came from another room. The two of them were face to face. How could two people be so different from each other?

He was one who had been out in the world. All suns had shone upon him. All winds had blown him on an interesting course. She, on the other hand, had never left home. She was neat and quiet. It seemed as if all her feelings had been held inside. Yet their faces had an expression that was very similar. They appeared to be very happy to see each other.

"Welcome home!" said Faith Egerton.

Cranfield did not answer her right away. His eye had been caught by a heart-shaped pin that Faith was wearing. Ralph remembered the stone of white quartz. He himself had carved it out of an Indian arrowhead that he had found. It was exactly the pattern of the heart worn by the maid in his dreams. When Cranfield had left the village ten years before, he had given the pin to Faith. As his parting gift to her, he had put it in a gold setting.

"So, Faith, you have kept the heart!" he said, finally.

"Yes," she said, blushing deeply. Then she asked, "And what else have you brought me from beyond the sea?"

"Faith!" replied Ralph Cranfield. "I have brought you nothing but a heavy heart! May I rest its weight on you?" These words poured out in a rush— almost as if he couldn't help himself.

"This heart, which I have worn so long, is the sign that you may," she answered. And as Faith said these words, she laid her trembling finger on the heart-shaped pin.

"Faith! Faith!" cried Cranfield, holding her in his arms. "You have made my wild and weary dream come true!"

Yes, the wild dream was awake at last. To find the mysterious treasure, Cranfield was to till the earth around his mother's house. He would find his riches there.

Instead of commanding people in a war—or as a king or a religious leader—he was to rule over the village children! And now the maid of his dreams had faded from his mind. In her place, he saw the playmate of his childhood.

Everyone who has such wild wishes should look nearby. Much contentment can be found close to home. Happy are those who find the answers without a weary world search, or a lifetime spent in vain!

An Old Woman's Tale

What would you see if you traveled backward in time? In this strange tale, David and Esther are witnesses to events that took place long ago. Why do these old-fashioned people look so familiar? Are they also visitors from another time in history?

IT WAS CLEAR THAT THEY WERE ARGUING ABOUT THE
CHURCH STEEPLE.

An Old Woman's Tale

A very old woman lived in the house where I was born. All day long she used to sit by the kitchen fire. She would keep her elbows on her knees and her feet in the ashes. Once in a while, she did some cooking. I remember that she always had a rough gray stocking in her lap. She was about halfway through knitting it. As the stocking grew closer to being done, she came closer to death. On the day she died, she had just knitted the last stitch.

The old woman would tell me stories at any time from morning till night. Sitting on a log of wood, I loved to listen to her mumbling voice. Her memory went back almost a hundred years. Stories of her own life were mixed up with those of many old people who had died when she was young. Based on these stories, you might have thought she lived during the time of Queen Elizabeth.

At least a thousand of her stories are stored in my mind. Some are more interesting than the one I am about to tell. Some are less interesting than this one, and others are not interesting at all. If I had the same kind of listener that she did, I would be happy to tell them all. But I am humble enough to know that I cannot tell a story as well as she could. Every one of her stories seemed interesting when she was telling them.

Her tales were usually about the place where she had been born, a village in

Connecticut. Because of her descriptions, that village came alive in my mind. In my imagination I could see it clearly. So I cannot tell you how happy I was to actually travel through that area about two years ago. As I looked at all the houses and the people, it seemed that a dream was coming to life.

One of the old woman's stories was about a one-hour sleep that all the villagers took at the same time. She never made it clear whether this happened once every 25, 50, or 100 years. But when that mysterious time arrived, everyone in the village slept. The minister snored over his half-written sermon, even though it was Saturday night and he needed the sermon in the morning. The mother's eyes closed as she bent over her child. The watcher at the bed of sickness slept, as did the dying person in the bed. To be sure, everyone in the village slept for that one hour. The old woman heard the story I am about to tell you from one of those villagers.

One summer evening, a young man and a young woman sat down together in the open air. They were distant cousins, and their family had once been wealthy. Now, the family was very poor. David wanted to ask Esther to marry him, but he couldn't even pay for the marriage license. On this particular evening, they were sitting in an open grove of elm and walnut trees. A spring of water bubbled up into the moonlight beside them.

The nearest house was some 20 yards away. It was the house in which their great-grandfather had lived. Even now it was a beautiful old house, with many high and narrow peaks. The roof was covered by creeping plants, which hung like curls on a wig.

The road in front of the house curved through the village. It was a wide road, divided in the middle by a lane of green plants. On each side was a grassy strip twice as wide as the road.

The houses along this road were a little odd. In the moonlight one house looked like a big pile of wood. This house was hiding behind a great thick tree. The lower story of the next house had sunk almost under the ground. It looked as if the poor little house had grown tired of the world and was trying to get away. Down the road stood one of the newer houses. Its painted face smiled boldly into the street. It looked as if it were proud of being the most beautiful house in the neighborhood.

The church was at the south end of the road. This was a dark, old barnlike building. It had a huge steeple, which had been added long after the church was built—50 years before. Past the church, the road wound down a hill and ended at the cemetery.

The young couple sat hand in hand under the trees. For several moments they had not spoken. The breeze was still, the brook barely bubbled, and the leaves had stopped moving. Everything lay still and silent. It was as if Nature were getting ready to sleep.

"What a beautiful night it is, Esther!" said David, somewhat sleepily.

"Very beautiful!" Esther agreed, in the same kind of voice.

"But how still!" continued David.

"Ah, too still!" said Esther, with a faint shudder, like a leaf when the wind kisses it.

And at that moment, they both fell asleep.

Perhaps because they were so alike, they both had the same dream. In their dream, they thought that they were still awake. They thought they were looking down the road at the old houses. They thought they were looking at the trees, whose branches almost reached into the windows of the houses. But there was a kind of mistiness over their minds. It was like the smoky air of an early fall night.

Then they began to notice that many people were either entering the village or already in the street. They couldn't tell where these people had come from. But certainly a crowd seemed to be gathering. Men, women, and children were all yawning and rubbing their eyes. They were stretching their arms and legs, and walking from one side of the road to the other. They seemed only half awake. Sometimes they stood still, with their hands over their brows to shade their eyes from the moonlight.

As Esther and David got closer, they saw that the people looked familiar. Their faces looked very much like families they knew in the village. Yet even though they looked familiar, there was not a single person whose exact face Esther and David had seen before.

Then the young couple noticed that all these people were wearing clothing that their great-grandparents might have worn. There was one figure who stood behind all the rest. This person was not close enough for Esther and David to see clearly.

"Where on earth, David, do all these odd people come from?" asked Esther. She almost felt like laughing.

"Nowhere on earth, Esther," said David, not knowing why he said so.

As they spoke, the strangers started to appear nervous. For a moment they looked toward the bubbling water before going on with what they were doing before. Then they all went to different parts of the village, as if they knew where they were going. Even though they were talking among themselves, Esther and David could hear neither their footsteps nor their voices.

Wherever there was an old house, 50 years old or more, a little group of these people gathered. Such groups were mostly made up of an old man and woman and some younger members of a family. Their faces were full of joy. They pointed out to each other the smallest things about the homes. It was as if they were comparing their memories with the real houses before them.

At some places along the road, there were deep, hollow spaces in the ground. These hollow spaces were overgrown with grass. Broken chimneys were the only sign that houses had once stood there. A few of the strangers sat at those places. The men folded their arms, too sad to speak. The women wrung their hands to show their sorrow. The little children fell to their knees, as if they were at a grave.

In some places, a new house had been built where an old one had once stood. There, a gray-haired man might be seen shaking a fist in anger at the new house. His old wife and their children seemed to join him in his anger. Such groups formed a fearful picture in the ghostly moonlight.

While these scenes were taking place, the lone figure in the rear of all the rest was walking down the road toward the mill. Then the eyes of David and Esther were drawn toward a young couple. The young man wore a sailor's uniform and the young woman was pale and slim. They met each other with a sweet hug in the middle of the street.

"How long it must be since they parted!" said David.

"Fifty years at least," said Esther.

Then they noticed several little groups of people who were talking among themselves. One group was seated on the grass near a store. The men in this group were an odd mix, indeed. One was a fine, fat, old fellow in shirt sleeves. He wore red trousers and a stained white apron, which he sometimes used to wipe his red face. Another man had the scar of an Indian tomahawk on his forehead. He looked like an old soldier—one who would never again answer the roll call. Another wore the hat and trousers of a sailor who had thrown away his youth upon the sea. He seemed only now to be returning, white-haired and weather-beaten, to his inland home. And there was also a thin young man, carelessly dressed. He kept looking sadly toward the pale young woman who was hugging the sailor in the street.

A man dressed for hunting was also there, along with one or two others. Then they were joined by a miller, who had walked up from the dusty mill. His coat was white with flour—as white as if it had been sprinkled with powdered starlight. All these people, except for the sad young man, were telling jokes and having fun. Their sides shook with laughter. Yet even at that, the men themselves looked like shadows flickering in the moonlight.

Four people, very different from these, stood in front of a large house. One was a little, old man. He was all dressed up in a three-cornered hat and sky-blue coat, both trimmed in gold. A coat of arms could be seen on his gold watch chain. Even though he was only about five feet tall, this little man seemed all pumped up with his own importance.

Next to the little man was a serious-looking person about 60 or 70 years old. His black suit and bald head were those of a famous preacher of the village. Fifty years before, he had spoken against wigs in a sermon. The two other men were dressed in dark gray. One was very tall and thin, and the other was short and fat. All four of these men talked with great energy. By the movements of their arms, it was clear that they were arguing about the church steeple. The old man in the gold-trimmed coat shook his cane angrily. As they argued, the figure in the background arrived from the mill. It proved to be an old woman carrying something in her hand.

"Why does she walk so slow?" asked David.

"Don't you see that she is lame?" asked Esther.

The woman now came closer to the rest of the group. David and Esther could see that her clothing was very grand. Her shoes were shiny, and her stockings had a design of gold clocks on them. She was wearing a red hoop-slip— so wide it looked like it would explode. Over this hoop-slip she wore a blue gown with a wide, stiff ruffle around the neck. She wore a fine cap and a pair of gold-rimmed glasses.

But the old lady's face was thin and sharp. She looked very stingy and greedy, as if she had saved every penny she ever had. Her face was an odd contrast to the beauty of her clothing. In her hand, she held an iron shovel, the kind that is used to clear the ashes out of the oven. Finding a spot in the ground between a walnut tree and the fountain, the old woman began to dig. But the dirt was as hard as rock.

Running out of breath, she threw down the shovel. She seemed very upset, and she wrung her thin yellow hands. Then, as if she had new hope, she tried to dig into the ground again. But the same thing happened. As David and Esther watched, the moonlight seemed to shine right through her and dance in the fountain behind her.

Then the little man in the gold-trimmed jacket happened to see her. He came up to her quietly, on tiptoe.

"How hard that old woman works!" said David.

"Go and help her, David," said Esther, kindly.

As David and Esther spoke, both the old woman and the fat little man lifted their eyes. For a moment, they looked at David and Esther with kindness and love. Then the old woman picked up the shovel again. She turned in surprise when a hand was suddenly put on her shoulder. But then she saw that it was the man in the blue coat. The two old people hugged each other in such a way that anyone would think they were married.

All this time, David and Esther saw that these figures were very ghostly. It was as if the gold on their clothing was made of the yellowest of the setting sunbeams. The blue in their clothing seemed to come from the dark sky near the moon. The man's silk vest was like the bright side of a fiery cloud, and the lady's red slip was like the blush of the morning sky. Both of them seemed to have come from colored air.

Suddenly there was a movement in the crowd. A man pulled out a watch as large as the clock on the famous steeple. He looked at the face of the clock, and then he left in a hurry. Everyone else left as quickly as possible behind him. Soon, all were gone. The wind rose up and followed them with a strange moaning down the lonely street.

Just *where* these people went is more than may be told. But David and Esther could now see only the shadowy figure of the old woman. She was standing in the moonlight at the graveyard gate, looking back toward the fountain.

"Oh, Esther! I have had such a dream!" cried David. In an instant he had snapped awake and was rubbing his eyes.

"And so have I!" answered Esther, with a surprised look on her face.

"It was about an old woman who had gold-rimmed glasses," said David.

"And a red hoop-slip," added Esther. They stared in each other's eyes, surprised and afraid at the same time. After a moment, David took a deep breath and stood up.

"If I live till tomorrow morning," he said, "I'll find out what is buried under that tree."

"And why not tonight, David?" asked Esther. She was a sensible woman, so she knew that it might be better to answer the question in secret.

David knew that Esther was right, and he looked around for something to dig with. He saw that the moon was shining brightly on something propped against the side of the old house. It was an old iron shovel that looked just like the one they had seen in their dreams! He had better luck with it than the old woman had. After he had dug a large hole, he poked his head down to the very bottom. "Oho!—what have we here?" cried David.

Thinking About
the Stories

The Birthmark

1. Which character in this story do you most admire? Why? Which character do you like the least?

2. How long ago was this story written? Think about the readers of that time. How were their lives different from the lives of today's readers? Was their purpose for reading the same or different? Were their tastes in reading the same or different? In what ways?

3. Suppose this story had a completely different outcome. Can you think of another effective ending for this story?

The Threefold Destiny

1. Who is the main character in this story? Who are one or two of the minor characters? Describe each of these characters in one or two sentences.

2. Does the main character in this story have an internal conflict? Does a terrible decision have to be made? Explain the character's choices.

3. Good writing always has an effect on the reader. How did you feel when you finished reading this story? Were you surprised, horrified, amused, sad, touched, or inspired? What elements in the story made you feel that way?

An Old Woman's Tale

1. Look back at the illustration that introduces this story. What character or characters are pictured? What is happening in the scene? What clues does the picture give you about the time and place of the story?

2. Suppose that this story was the first chapter in a book of many chapters. What would happen next?

3. What period of time is covered in this story—an hour, a week, several years? What role, if any, does time play in the story?